POETRY BY RUTH SILCOCK

Mrs. Carmichael
A Wonderful View of the Sea

Ruth Silcock

Biographies etc.

ANVIL PRESS POETRY

Published in 2006
by Anvil Press Poetry Ltd
Neptune House 70 Royal Hill London SE10 8RF
www.anvilpresspoetry.com

This book is published with financial assistance
from Arts Council England

Designed and set in Monotype Dante by Anvil
Printed and bound in England
by Cromwell Press, Trowbridge, Wiltshire

ISBN 0 85646 383 3

A catalogue record for this book
is available from the British Library

This book is for my sister Diana,
who has taken part in many of the poems

ACKNOWLEDGEMENTS

Some of these poems have been published in *Dark Horse, Literature & Aesthetics, The Rialto, Smiths Knoll* and *THE SHOp*.

Thank you to certain people who have helped me, two of whom will find themselves in this book. Thanks to the librarians of Crawley Library in Sussex for supplying me with copies of documents. Also very grateful thanks to the founder and trustees and staff of Hawthornden International Retreat for Writers, and to my fellow writers there for conversation and exploration. It was a wonderful, as well as useful, four weeks. Several of these poems were written or completed at Hawthornden, in the spring of 2004.

CONTENTS

THE WALKING TOUR

Joy, on a walking tour in a foreign forest,
Tripped from a root or fell from a crag, and died.
Days later her Executors, the Bank,
Rang the sad news to the next-of-kin, who cried
At such a desolate death on a far hillside –
Out of doors, in the dark perhaps, no family near.
While we were laughing, they said, was poor Joy dying
On her own, as she always was, with her pain and her fear?

They wanted to pay their last respects, to fly
To France for the funeral, to stand by her grave,
To pack her things and to pay her bills and to burn
Her letters, and search for anything special to save.
Most of all, they said, they just wanted a chance to behave
As families do, and forget the past, and grieve.
But the Bank and the Embassy were shut for Easter,
All ferries and flights on strike, so they could not leave.

And after all, they said, she died long ago,
She carefully killed any love we had held in our heart.
Far forests for her were safer than gardens at home
Since people in England look odd if they wander apart
And she was less lost when she went, without guidebook
     or chart,
To countries where every foreigner seems the same,
Where language is nonsense, all British behaviour bizarre,
And being abroad is adventure and therefore not shame.

So, stiff in black jersey and long black skirt, she would march
Up and down in the woods, roundabout, in pursuit of a track,
Hair piled on her head, long hands in the thickest black gloves,
Long narrow white face, closed narrow grey lips, poker back.
When Joy first decided on travel, she chose to wear black,
She renounced all her sins, which she blamed on a mischievous
    friend,
She renounced all her love, which she gave to a little dead
    dog,
And then shriven and clean she could wander through France
    to her end,

Which was loving of her. She had spared them her passion
    and hate.
They were none of them poisoned or stabbed or divorced or
    embraced.
They jogged on for years in an easy and leisurely way,
Thanks to her, all their anguish was normal. She never dis-
    graced
Their name, or their trust in each other. The only sad waste
Was her own living death in a maze of dark woods, far from
    home.
We kept following, calling, they said, but she never replied.
And so they could rest in their grief. She was too kind to
    come.

THE ORPHAN

'I'm an orphan,' the giant Kiwi says,
'I'm an orphan.'
Three of us in Economy Class, side by side for twenty-four
    hours,
And the middle one
Is the orphan.
Huge hands and feet, huge shoulders and thighs,
The vast orphan
Is taking up half my seat, and I'm crushed
Flat on the window, I might be a butterfly,
By the orphan.

The man on the left has been sprawled in the aisle
By the elbowing orphan
Who is telling the back of the seat in front of him
'I'm an orphan.'
His mother's passed on, his father's now gone,
And there's no-one,
No-one to meet him or greet him or welcome him
Home,
Monumental sad orphan
Who is bending across me to look at the clouds – Ouch! –
My ribs!
Please be careful, great orphan.

The chap on the left is shoved into a drinks trolley –
'My mistake, sorry –'. Hauled back. 'Let me buy you a –
Just wasn't thinking and –' lost in his loneliness,
Towering between us, what can small people
(Tattered and battered and bruised and resentful) –

What can we do for this heartbroken hero?
I remember,
I am an orphan.
The man on the left whose feet have been trodden on –
Is he also an orphan?
Is even the pilot an orphan?

We both try to comfort our mammoth man-mountain,
Over the continents, over the oceans,
New Zealand, North Island – Auckland below us!
Anyone down there who knows him?

Two pigmies are guiding through Passports and Customs
A skyscraping earthshaking cloudpiercing sorrowing
Orphan towards – is it nothing? and nobody?
Will it be desolation?
– Thank God, here they come, a crowd of colossal
Welcoming Kiwis who claim him, embrace him,
Clap his back, smother him, tears.
He'll be O.K.

The chap from the left and myself from the right
Are stretching and sighing and flexing and breathing –
How's your spine? How's your neck? Try some
    knee-bending?
We're full-sized humans again –
Except that wherever we look there are giants
(What can they feed them on? Is it the ice-cream?)
And far far away, like a grove of tall trees,
We can just spot our orphan and family – laughing?
We limp out into the light.

THE VICAR OF NINETY

The Vicar of ninety
Rides a bicycle,
Panting up hillsides,
Dashing down.

The Vicar of ninety's
Eyes are like bullets,
Head like a cannonball.
Fingers crack.

The Vicar of ninety,
Brave and athletic,
Vaults the school wall
To flatten a bully.

        ★

The Vicar is also
Scholastic, dramatic.
He's teaching me Greek
Though we both prefer stories

Of silhouette families
Framed on his wallpaper,
Schooldays at Marlborough,
Cambridge, the river –

        ★

The Vicar of ninety,
Remembering rivers,
Has asked me and mother
To travel first-class.

He wears a white jacket,
White shoes and white waistcoat,
Yellowing flannels,
A Panama hat,

And he bows as he hands us
Into the swaying
Boat on the water.
He rows like a demon

But puffs and goes scarlet.
My mother takes over.
We eat in a field.
– The Vicar rows home

Slowly, on sparkling
Wavelets, a flower
In his buttonhole nodding.
He snores in the train.

                *

The Vicar of ninety
Taught me no Greek
But made me tell fortunes
At the church fête

And he lent me his precious
Classical Dictionary
(Ancient Mythology)
(Dusty and heavy).

*

At Christmas the children
Sat round his pulpit,
At Easter – a prophet,
Arms lifted – he bellowed

'Good News! Christ is risen!'
We all cheered inside us.
Now he's dead, and I've given
Away his great book.

SEYMOUR STREET

Someone quite near me spoke to me –
Someone beside my feet –
Crouched on the kerb in the evening street
Requesting a light and a cigarette
A small old lady sat.

Ten minutes, she asked, of company?
Just out of hospital,
Now with no friends at all,
Just musical instruments
And herself, in her flat.

There were grand pianos mostly,
In three long rooms, crowded.
'Coffee?' she asked, among shrouded
Masses of instruments
Attending our chat.

AFON FACH

Written in thanks to Mrs. Sylvia Parry,
for her kindness on a wet evening.

At the back of beyond
At Cricieth Station
Trains late
Shops closing
No taxis
Clouds looming
Sylvia Parry
Saved the day.

Sylvia Parry
Showed me a shop
Rang for a taxi –
No taxi
Rain falling
Sylvia Parry
Picked up my bags
And drove me here.

Without Mrs. Parry
– No food
Cupboards bare
At Afon Fach.

Without Mrs. Parry
– Soaking wet
Where to dry clothes
At Afon Fach?

Without Mrs. Parry
– Worn out
However to find
This Afon Fach?

Such thankfulness
To Sylvia Parry
Who saved the day
At the back of beyond
And brought me to beautiful
Afon Fach.

THE WALKERS

She sees them walk up the hill and out of the mist
With the dogs ahead.

She opens her eyes.
There are jobs to be done, there are many good friends
     nearby.

She sees them walk up the hill, with the dogs ahead.

TWO NANNIES

Rebecca

'Don't walk with one foot on the pavement and one in
    the gutter –
Just look at Rebecca –
A car ran over her foot that was in the gutter,
And see how it's wrecked her –
You're sorry now, but it's what you deserved,
You foolish Rebecca.'

Robin

Pale, frail Robin,
White face, pointed chin,
Dark eyes and skinny legs –
What is wrong with him?

Is it his great big Nanny,
Overshadowing him?
Is it her bedtime stories?
Is that what's wrong with him?

She says that a sharp steel needle
Was lost below Robin's white skin
And it's travelling, travelling,
Until it finishes him.

THE WORTHIES OF ALDEBURGH TOWN

We're the Worthies of Aldeburgh Town,
We're glad that we've brought it renown
– The future should know
That we strove long ago
To bring honour to Aldeburgh Town.

Should our fame be from painting or pen?
People don't forget pictures. – Next then,
Our debate on the fee.
Write it down, carefully,
Nineteen heads, most with hats, and all men.

Our artist had always used sheets
To cover his wall, but his seats
And space were so crowded,
His old wall was shrouded
With sailcloth. It hangs like a treat.

The hardest part was, to decide
Who should sit at the top? At the side?
Those two at the front
(Law and Vicar) were blunt
And seized the best seats in their pride.

Every man sports his hat, except one.
(Our town's known to be cold, lacking sun.)
I'll wager you'll guess
From their headgear and dress
Who can teach, who can fish, hold a gun?

We've a butcher and baker (no squire),
There's the choir-master (soon to retire),
A weaver, a tailor,
And many a sailor,
And our MAYOR, a good man we admire.

We don't know why the artist has lined
All our heads into rows, which inclined
Our eyes to look far
At the future? A star?
I'm thinking it's time that we dined.

We're the Worthies of Aldeburgh Town,
Our faces are weathered and brown,
We work early and late
To keep Aldeburgh great.
We're grim, but we're proud of our town.

CLAIRE

We never did care
For Claire,
Her blue stare,
How it pleased her to scare
Any new girl. – Despair
Followed Claire.

Yet our teachers would care
For Claire,
Her blue stare
And the wave of her hair.
No-one else could compare
With their Claire.

Now we don't need to care
About Claire –
But those people who sat in her dentist's chair,
Watching her drill and her bright blue stare –
Did they share our despair?
Or did no-one else ever compare
With their Claire?

VICTOR

Where's Victor? they said,
Why doesn't Victor come
For his regular Thursday appointment?
He isn't at home

And nobody can find him.
Where is Victor? they said,
– The last of seven brothers
Six of whom chose to be dead.

We couldn't save the others.
How can poor Victor bear
To live in the house without them?
They searched for him everywhere.

After a week they found him
Sitting under a tree
On the river-bank, with his hat on his head,
In his brothers' company.

HENRY

I had a boyfriend once
Who never cut his toenails
Which therefore had grown
(Shiny and hard and brown)
Right over his toes,
And begun – because of his shoes I suppose –
To curve quite neatly backwards
Towards the soles of his feet.

We somehow drifted apart
But from time to time I've wondered,
Where are his toenails now?
Have they reached the ball, the arch?
Have they continued
Steadily round the heel of the foot,
And then aimed upwards
To ankle, even to calf?

One thing I know about Henry,
He would never allow his toenails
The least little fraction above the crook in his knees,
For how could he sit down?
He was a man who liked comfort.

FRIENDS

Boarding-school.
Two friends who
Held hands, sang.
Gates went clang.

Off they went,
Long years spent
Hands together,
Any weather.

One friend older,
One friend colder?
Meets another –
Friend or lover?

Old friend tragic –
End of magic –
Hands half-parted,
Noble-hearted

Old friend sighs
Blessing, dies,
Glad for others –
Happy lovers

Two friends swing
Arms, hands. Sing
Till one's older,
Next grows colder.

BY THE FIRE

We were sitting in armchairs beside the fire
When I suddenly noticed that you were now standing
On some sort of boat – or was it a raft? –
And were waving and calling and floating and drifting –
Drifting slowly away –

Away over water your voice sounded fainter,
Your waving was weaker, the sea was now rushing
And speeding to oceans, and you were so small
And I can't hear your call, and your arms – I can't see them –
And that tiny speck on the distant horizon –
It's gone.

IN THE SUITCASE

In the suitcase
Held by a paper-clip,
Top copy
Of a typed love story.

In the suitcase,
Held by several paper-clips,
Carbon copies
Of typed love letters.

At the bottom of the suitcase,
Torn by rusty paper-clips,
Pages yellowed pages
Of scrawled and loving letters.

A FIGURE OF SPEECH

Some people say 'basket case'
As dramatic expression!
Suppose you or I were a basket case?
We might feel depression
Deep and long
Might even feel a hatred for the strong
Whole healthy hearty people
Who'd use a rescued body in a basket
To make a good impression.

THE BIRTHDAY PARTY

She was twenty-one on the fourth of August,
Fourth of August nineteen fourteen.
She'd planned to have such a lovely party
But all the young men went missing. They'd been
Enlisting, they said, her two brothers and one
Friend who till then had seemed quite keen.
Off they went in their uniforms.
Back they came in nineteen eighteen.
None of the young men missing, though all
Altered. The eldest, wounded, was seen
In no-man's-land. They had dragged him back.
The second was saved by the Bible between
Bullet and heart (his brother's gift).
The third, the friend who had seemed so keen,
Was deafened and dulled, and the sister said
She'd rather not marry now, it would mean
Not much fun, too late to become
Twenty-one in nineteen eighteen.

THE RESCUE

Our father never forgave
The person who came to save
His body from where it lay on the peaceful river bed.

AFTER THE SERVICE

If we stand on tiptoe
By the churchyard wall,
If we hold the railings
If we do not fall
We can see a butler
Masked in evergreen
Creeping down the hillside,
Shy of being seen.

Watch the curious butler,
Black and pinstriped, cling
To each tomb and treetrunk.
That's a piece of string
Dangling from his finger,
Tied around a box,
Small and white – for cakes? – but
Somehow something shocks.

Black and pinstriped butler
Slides and slithers near,
Stops beside the railings –
Why do we feel fear?
Drops a large white hanky,
Kneels upon the ground,
Like a dog starts digging,
Glancing all around.

Takes a tiny penknife,
Cuts the string in two,
Bends above his box and –
Pinstripes hide our view.
He's jumped up, he's stamping,
Smoothing – wiping clean
Penknife, shoes and kneecaps,
Hoping no-one's seen.

This man is no butler.
Now he strolls around,
Wipes his face and gazes
Over holy ground,
Wipes his eyes politely
With his handkerchief,
Nods to let us know he's
Just interred our grief.

MURIEL

We are sorting her chest of drawers –
This for me, This for you, This was so much hers –
'I'll never have a friend like that again.'
We are meeting the jaunty lawyer
And signing his forms and discussing the weather.
'I'll never have a friend like that again.'

She used to play cards at this table,
Now it's covered with cake-crumbs after the funeral.
'I'll never have a friend like that again.'
We wash cups in the broken sink
And it's time to go and she rings me. 'I think
I'll never have a friend like that again.'

And now it's winter and snow,
She's no light, she's no heat, she is ill, did I know
She'll never have a friend like that again?
She spent Christmas with cousins, she died there.
I cannot remember her face, but I hear
'I'll never have a friend like that again.'

· AN ENGLISHMAN'S LOVE SONG

Come here my love, and sit by me,
We'll love each other until tea.
You'll keep my heart and body warm
While I will try to shield from harm
As much of you as I can hold –
I think the tea is growing cold.

MALANGALI

In Africa, aged five,
I found myself in bush as tall as forest
Where a giant pig,
Pink, bristling and ferocious,
Saw and pursued me
To the top of a little hill where the trees ended.

A row of soldiers,
Scarlet, with white pith helmets, blew gold bugles
While the Union Jack
Was slowly lowered from its high white pole
Across the orange sunset,
Purple landscape,
Into the night.

THE COAT

Once, as a child,
I came out of church and followed
My mother's long brown coat.
For miles I followed
Until the head
At the top of the long coat turned.
The grey and horrid head glared down upon me.
It wasn't mother's.
What had they done with mother?
The strange and horrid head
Bent close beside me.
'Stop following me, you silly child,
Go home!'
I stared at mother's coat that had misled me,
Even the streets were changed, and all the people,
The sea invisible,
Only the friendly gasworks gave me comfort.
The lady in my mother's coat soon dragged me
Back down the hill to church and children, mother.
I saw the two long coats stand side by side,
I saw the angry head on top of each,
And one was mother's.

THANK GOD FOR ARTHUR RANSOME

My mother was always busy.
Once, when I was ill,
She sent me away to stay
With Granny and Grandpa,
And the minute that I arrived
My Granny confiscated
Every one of my comics.
She said that comics were bad,
They would make me over-excited.
I was so bored!

My bedroom was very narrow
(Its name was the Prophet's Chamber)
And the shelves beside my bed
Were filled with billions of books,
Each of them written by Granny.
So I read most of her books
(All about bringing up children),
And I liked some of the stories,
Especially the naughty children.
But all the red books were the same,
Also the brown and white ones,
And then, in one of her books,
Granny said to a Nanny
That she should whip a child.
So I stopped reading Granny.

My Grandpa was a doctor,
He was once a children's doctor.

He was very old. He had
A whole room full of books.
So I decided to read
Grandpa's books. One day
When my grandparents had gone out
I borrowed some of Grandpa's
Rather large books.
It was awful. All of his books
Were full of scary pictures
Of naked children standing
Beside big chairs.
Some children had swollen stomachs
And crooked arms and legs
And one had a huge round head
That one day might fall off.
Snap went his neck.
Another thing was, the poor children
Without any clothes on, were glaring
Out of the page at me.
I didn't like it.

So I stopped reading books
And started to talk to the flies
But Granny said they were dirty.

Then one wonderful day they fixed up,
From their sitting-room downstairs,
A loudspeaker in my bedroom.
I could listen to Children's Hour,
Uncle Mac and the Zoo Man
And Toy Town, and lots of plays,
And two detectives.

After that came the news,
Football results and weather,
And they were O.K..
But later, my light was turned off
And Granny and Grandpa downstairs
Always seemed to be listening
To some doctor talking of illness
And some people dying.
Also next door you see,
My Great-Aunt was slowly dying.

Which is why I thanked God for Toy Town,
Thanked God for the sensible Aunt
Who brought me some decent books,

Especially Arthur Ransome.

'HEALTHY GROWTH'

(the title of one of my Grandfather's books)

Grandfather's grail was healthy growth
For people and trees – he loved them both –
He cured children's rickets with fresh air and sun,
Exercise, oranges, till they could run.
They learnt to breathe deeply, their bodies were straight –
And when Grandpa was old, and it was too late
For him to help people, he looked after trees,
Clearing out brambles, curing disease,
Giving more light, more space, more air –
The trees grew straight under grandfather's care.

BESIDE THE SEA

We lived by the sea –
A haze of blue in summer,
Crowds everywhere

With deckchairs, donkeys,
Buckets and spades, sandcastles,
A Punch and Judy.

No room to picnic,
We ate upright, on pebbles,
Sandy sandwiches

Then splashed into waves
Full of pink limbs, heads bobbing.
Strange faces spluttered.

    ★

Our sea in winter,
Our emptiness, grey ocean,
Moved rocks and shingle.

Its waves crashed railings,
It reared over promenades,
It roared past houses.

'Did it reach your road?'
'We saw yellow foam floating
Over our doorstep.'

And there were stories
Of dogs, even people, snatched
And grabbed by great tides

Which tore them from land,
Sucked them and flung them, drowned them.
Not heard of again.

*

Once, perhaps midnight,
Our mother woke us, dressed us,
Led us through dark storm

To a great black shape
Beached on the shoreline, gleaming.
Our torches showed us

Bit by bit, a long
Leathery living body.
People were carving

Initials in it.
Someone said, 'All whales belong
To the King. Send it

By train to London.'
Others said 'If it's living,
A vet is needed.'

No-one knew. We stood
In the rain and stroked our whale.
The torches flickered.

By the next morning
The whale was smaller, greyer,
And carved all over.

WHEN I WAS TWELVE

When I was twelve, and crying,
I found that tears were salty,
I found that tears could make rainbows
If I blurred my eyes.
Suddenly, here was science,
Also, here was creation –
I tried to cry again,
To recover the world.

FATHER'S GIRLFRIENDS

Half your girlfriends were always in tweeds,
With porkpie hats and sensible shoes,
They strode about, they were brisk and blunt,
But weren't they unusual women to choose

When the other half of your girlfriends were young?
In fact they were always twenty-four –
Since the slender redheads, the buxom blondes,
By twenty-five were too old to adore.

You took us to stay with the women in tweeds
Who were mostly firm and not much fun –
But how we longed for the redheads and blondes
Who flashed through our lives like the summer sun,

Kingfishers, humming-birds, whizzing by,
How we enjoyed the games and the play!
– Until we too became twenty-five
And knew you'd be asking if you could stay.

THE BOSS

*(to be sung to the tune of 'The Daring Young Man
on the Flying Trapeze')*

Whenever the talk turns to murder, I see
The Boss standing there and looking at me
From under the brim of his Trilby hat. He
Thinks he's so smart. He's a spiv.

He fancies himself in his camel-hair coat,
Wide shoulders, and collar turned up round the throat.
I can't see his face, just his eyes, and I note
Not the colour, the stare that they give.

I'd just been demobbed, I needed a job.
The pay was O.K., and I wasn't a snob.
The factory's fine if I don't have to swab
Those filthy old floors at night.

When you came in to work there were gates and a yard
Full of barrels, weeds, rubbish – the stink! – but no guard.
We girls went upstairs, the work wasn't hard,
Though the fellows downstairs weren't polite!

Our job was to finish posh radio sets
While we listened to music and songs I forget –
Then two of us raced – it was piece-work – we'd bet
We'd earn more – the Charge Hand said No.

She called in the Boss who lived somewhere in town.
He kept looking at us, and we kept looking down.

All we could see was those eyes – not a frown –
We were sacked, and were eager to go.

A very kind uncle gave me a large note
Which covered clothes, lodging and Paris and boat.
I was trying to read a French paper, remote
From home. – 'That's the Boss's Yard!'

That yard full of barrels and rubbish and weeds,
Our factory where we were sacked for misdeeds,
Where our mates might be working while I tried to read
Through the French which was stumbling and hard.

It seemed that the Boss liked high living, and so
He killed women for money and jewels, he'd stow
Their bodies in barrels of acid, and go
With their forged names to show at the Bank.

He thought he'd escape, but his science was poor,
Bodies may vanish, but not handbags, nor
False eyelashes, fingernails, all remained for
Police to search barrels that stank.

The Boss left his notebook with lists of names who
Were all women with money (such a little would do).
Everyone knew them – I might be there too
If I hadn't been given the sack.

WORKING FOR WORLD PEACE

For two and a half days
I worked for World Peace
In a high and silent building,
Warm and still.

Footsteps were lost in carpets,
Voices faded in whispers,
Hushed and humble people
Paled into walls.

Everyone cared for peace
Quietly, fought for peace
Gently, ambitious for peace
In a diffident way.

We typists had to type
On silent typewriters,
Which meant electric, brand new
In those dove-like days.

But I could only hammer
Hard on the keys like a hailstorm,
Dashing off brilliant speeds,
Nonsensical, breakneck.

There were tentative offers of help,
Baffled apologies.
I fled to the noise in the street.
They sent a large cheque.

BOOTS

I look at my boots that have walked
Today on the shore
Over pebbles and tough grass and trash
And now wait by the door
Like dogs that are eager to go –
My two boots say to me
Please use us a few times more
Before we are free.

THE PERILS OF AGEING

Faster and faster the sledge travels over the snow,
Louder and louder the wolves are howling – we know
That we'll have to throw somebody out – and while the
    wolves feed
We can whip up the horses – our only hope is their speed.

But the night is still dark and the horses are tired and we hear
The distant howling of wolves once again coming near
And someone else must be thrown to the wolves – we all
    know
That soon it will be our turn to be flung on the snow.

PARROT

My pet, my parrot
Has flown to the dark forest,
The savage forest.

There will be foxes
And birds of prey, and hunters
Eager to shoot him.

We've crossed the river,
We've called him through the gorges,
Searched caves and thickets.

My silly parrot,
What will he find to eat there?
And where will he sleep?

We've scattered peanuts
Along the trails, to woo him.
Poor hungry parrot.

Windows are open,
Lights shine across the water,
His favourite words

Are shouted loudly –
Sadly we go home, sighing
Poor parrot is lost.

You wicked parrot!
You sinful, heartless parrot!
Asleep in your cage!

Shut doors and windows!
Lock up his cage! Oh parrot,
Talk to me, kiss me.

KOMODO DRAGONS

1   *They Meet Other Dragons*

'And did you really see the dragons of Komodo?'
        'Yes, they were just large lizards.'
'With your own eyes you saw the dragons of Komodo?'
        'Yes, they were ugly, stinking.'
'And you have proof you saw the dragons of Komodo?'
        'I have these smudgy pictures,
Snapshots of ugly, stinking, large, ferocious lizards.'

'The dragons will be green and scarlet, yellow,
Scaly and serpentine, and flying, writhing –
Some climb the sky by piling clouds together,
Some dive below the waters, coil in whirlpools.
They move in mists, they increase torrents, guarding
Our homes from harm, and sending rain to save us.
Dragons have horns and claws and bulging eyeballs
And some shoot fire, and most own pearls, and always
They have the gift of changing their appearance –
Commonly choosing human shape, assuming
The look of someone like yourself – a bearded,
A heavy gentleman who sits in comfort.'

        'It's just a name, just dragons.'

        'Thank you for introductions
        to dragons from Komodo.'

2   Two of Them Meet the Tourists

'I've a coat of heavy armour
And a hood made out of chainmail
And I waddle when I'm walking
But I'm very quick at running
And if I sniff I'll find you
And if I catch I'll eat you
For my tongue's a dripping ribbon
Which is flickering with hunger."

'My appetite's enormous
But because I'm huge and clumsy
I must sneak up on my dinner
And then bite at it with poison.
As a mother I am faithful
To my eggs. I gobble children.
We're disgusting, yet you cherish
Your last living, loathsome dragons.'

FALLING AWAKE

I was falling awake, but it wasn't what I had expected –
Not that crash on the floor with the bed overhead like one
    of the white cliffs of Dover,
Not the tick of the clock saying time to get up it's Monday
    now Tuesday now Wednesday,
Not a nightmare behind me but no bones are broken I'm
    real and alive and quite normal,
Nor even the opposite, rising asleep to bright dreams of
    sky-flying and swimming –

No,

At first it didn't seem falling at all nor waking but closer
    to felling,
Tree-felling chopped trunks into matchsticks and tooth-
    picks and where is the forest, green forest?
And fell as in fate as in fells as cold moors in the winter
    when daylight is fading –
Will I ever get home and then will there be home and fell
    is more final than falling.

(We do not like thee, Dr. Fell, you've once again ruined
    the picnic.)

But

Falling and falling, awake wide awake, top speed such a
    hurtling and howling
From the rush through the air, toytown looming huge,
    worms and mice cry aloud, and the future

Is suddenly still and clear as a crystal so precious don't harm
 it, let's save it
From seas without fish and skies without birds and land with
 no animals – us?

Such an effort –

There's time to climb back into bed,
Shut my eyes, drowse under blankets,
Dream of arising asleep into flying,
How peaceful –

A parachute hangs from a tree in the breeze, swaying in
 safety, not falling

'CHINESE WORKERS ENJOY A NEW PROSPERITY'

A square grey room,
Six upright chairs,
A lightbulb hanging,
A refrigerator.

No carpet on the floor,
No curtains at the window,
One picture on the wall,
A refrigerator.

A woman in blue
Has a birchbroom in her hand.
There's a bucket and a sink
And the woman is smiling

As the rain pours down
On a man in blue
With a group of tourists
Sheltered in the doorway.

The woman in blue
In the middle of the room
(One picture on the wall,
A lightbulb hanging)

Is holding out her hand
To the smiling guide and tourists
To show them her white, shining,
Gigantic refrigerator.

AN ARTIST PAINTS SYDNEY

A woman sits at an easel,
Painting Sydney –
The harbour, the beaches, the bush,
Small birds and flowers,
A kangaroo, a koala –
But somehow she's missed out,
Avoided deleted forgotten,
The city of Sydney.

TALL POPPIES

In our country
We've never liked tall poppies.
We prefer
Flat level fields of short red poppies bringing
No shade, no shadow, only
An equal joy on summer afternoons.

TRAVELLERS

Last week at the back of the Downs,
Out blackberrying,
I saw in the distance a bus,
Heard dogs barking.
Travellers.
I climbed over a broken fence
And walked by the edge of dusty fields –
'A quicker way home' said my pretence,
Escaping from Travellers.

THE TWO-MILE WALK

I woke one summer morning, keen to walk.
My friends all praised the track beside the river –
'Only two miles,' they said, 'between two bridges,
And on the way you'll see a ruined castle,
Half lived in, so we've heard. Follow the path,
And just above you'll find the strangest chapel.'

Eager to see the famous, ancient chapel,
Ready with boots, stick, maps, I planned my walk.
The sunny day, the birdsong, woodland path,
Soon led me to a small and sparkling river –
Only – I'd somehow lost the ruined castle
And found a Country Park, a brook, wrong bridges.

A kindly keeper spoke of other bridges
Over the hilltops, near a distant chapel,
Beside a pink and ruined, far-off castle.
'Taxi'? he asked. I told him I would walk!
And marched away to find the ruins, river,
Making a few mistakes, but found the path.

Jaw set, I climbed the hilltops. A new path
Led down towards our rushing river, bridges
(One far, one near). I crossed, and heard the river
Roar under me. Now steep steps, marked 'To Chapel'.
Panting, I reached a crossroads. Was my walk
Half over now? Success! There was the castle!

'Danger' the sign said, near the ruined castle.
I wanted safety, chose the dusty path.
The chapel sold me tea and cake. The walk
Seemed easy now – just river, and its bridges –
And scorning danger, grateful to the chapel,
I slid downhill. – Was my path up the river?

Or was my way the dangerous, down river?
I set my back against the ruined castle,
Shook out, read upside down, my maps – the chapel,
Its calm and peace behind me now. My path
Was marked 'unsafe' between the two old bridges.
Tall trees, ravines and dusk obscured my walk.

I won't forget that river's rocky path,
The blood-red sunset castle. Give me bridges!
Only those prayers in chapel saved that walk!

IT IS ALL BECOMING UNKNOWN

The father says yes,
I have a Gillian too.
She's much younger than you.
How strange
That your and my Gillian both seem to share the same name.

The mother says yes,
I know both your ages – I'll guess
That you must be thirty-eight?
And then you're thirty-six? Am I right?
Two elderly daughters accept with delight,
And everyone's pleased.

Dead, says the mother, all dead,
As she looks at the snow and the leafless trees.
Dead dead in the sitting-room where she sees
White-headed people, ghostly and frail in their chairs.
The daughter says 'winter – remember the winter, then
        summer?
In summer the trees will be covered with leaves,
New green leaves.'

THE DOCTOR

'Your time is up,' the doctor said.
'You haven't found a home?
You know your mother must be safe
Before her mind has gone?
You say you've looked? The Homes are full?
Expensive? Distant? Bare?
You think that you can pick and choose?
Just go and find somewhere.

You waste this conference's time.
– Your mother's rich, they say?
Not so? Don't argue. Understand,
Your mother cannot stay.
Our Day Centre is crowded, crammed,
There are no beds to spare.
Don't dawdle, act. And don't come back.
Find somewhere, anywhere.

THE RIGHT HOME

'Do you think that the Park would be right for you?'
'Oh no, it was much too cold.'
'And how about Pilgrims? Would that do?'
'Everyone looked so old.'

'The place with the pillars and polished hall?'
'They were all so chilly and grand
And nobody smiled or asked my name
And nobody took my hand.'

'They were chatting away at Chestnut Lodge –'
'Too softly for me to hear,'
'The Willows had wonderful sofas and chairs –'
'But none of the staff came near.'

'St. Faith's?' 'Too dirty, a dirty cup
Of luke-warm slops for tea.'
'St. Agnes?' 'Silent. Silent and still –
All dead, dead dead to me.

The home that I like the best of all
Is my own. If I can't stay here
Then take me away to the place I beg –
In the south – near trains – somewhere –

I remember it smells and the carpets are worn
And everyone seemed to be free
And busy, with jokes, and there seemed to be hope –
But its name has forsaken me.'

THE BROOM CUPBOARDS

The broom cupboards doubled
As visitors' loos.
We always felt troubled
By broom cupboards doubled
With plumbing. Pipes bubbled
And steam hid our views
Of the broom cupboards, doubled
As visitors' loos.

CONTENTMENT

A cosy old lady reclined
On two soft, snow-white pillows – 'I find
That my pink eiderdown
And rose-red dressing gown
Keep me happy, contented, refined.'

NINE YORKSHIRE POEMS

1 *Cows*

The car's windows
Are covered with sticky, silvery,
Licks from cows' broad tongues
Gathering salt.

2 *The Haunted House*

That house over there,
That house is home to a ghost.
They've changed that house inside,
Raised ceilings and floors,
But the ghost still haunts his home,
Legs dangling through the ceiling,
Trunk and grey head advancing
On the upstairs carpet.

3   *The Greedy Dog*

Once, walking the Yorkshire moors
In sunshine, with heather and bogs,
We sat on some rocks, for a picnic
With a greedy dog.

Then travelled for cheerful miles
Till the bright day turned cold,
White fog on the moors.
We were lost, but the dog

Led us back to the rocks,
Gobbled up crumbs of sandwich,
And eager for afternoon tea
Hurried us home.

4   *Heptonstall and Hebden Bridge*

Heptonstall
Is interesting, but small –
If you want crumpets or fish and chips or woolly
        socks or medicated hair shampoo or non-stick
        saucepans or an electric cooker or a 'fridge,
Choose Hebden Bridge.

5   *The Earnest Artist*

An earnest artist
Painting in a meadow
Felt her audience
Becoming too eager.

On turning round, she found
Some interested cows
Blowing their warm breath
Softly down her neck.

6   *Pub Lunch*

One small and chilly town
Only had three pubs,
Only one pub did lunch,
Which was Chilli con Carne.

'You'll have to wait,' we were told.
The landlady disappeared
And reappeared wearing boots
Lugging a large white tub.

She left by another door
And after a while poked her head
Round the door to announce
That our lunch was defrosting.

There were sounds of hammering,
And when she returned, looking weary,
We asked if she had any bread?
'The boy's took it for bait, for his fishing.'

7   *The Street Sweeper*

In Howarth there's a roaring storm,
The street-sweeper still sweeps,
Whatever leaves come near his broom
Are tidied into heaps

That fly before the next great blast.
He sweeps them up again,
He's found one sodden leaf alone
And saves it from the rain.

The gutter's full. He cleans it out.
We shelter somewhere warm
And two hours later find him here
Still sweeping in the storm.

8   *The Black Bull*

We've come to the famous Black Bull
To shelter from weather. It's full,

And everyone's jolly and warm
Now that the storm can't harm.
One gloomy fellow's alone,
Down-at-heel, woebegone –
He tells my kind sister his life,
About the death of his wife.
He feels better for speaking, he thinks,
So he wants to buy us all drinks
And he's cheering up now while I pay
For the next round – he whispers away
To my sister. He's asked for her hand
In marriage. He knows he's not grand
But steady. She thanks him, explains
That she's married, can't marry again,
But she knows he's a good, upright man.
We shake hands, say goodbye in the rain.

9   *Christmas in Yorkshire*

Christmas in Yorkshire,
Striding on top of white hedges,
Leaping from wall to wall –
Even a fall
On the softest mattress of all
Can't do very much harm
In this new world of snowballs and sledges.

THE SILENT WOMAN

The Inn was The Silent Woman.
We asked the landlord why?
'Why do you think? You women
Are always talking, but I

Like this place to be quiet.
There's plenty of work to do.'
'But why was the woman silent?'
'If I tell, that'll silence you. –

She was dead. Maybe somebody killed her,
And maybe it gave him peace.
Maybe you'll not be wanting
To sleep where someone's deceased?'

TRACEY'S NEST

'Who comes knocking at my door?'
'I am your new helper, for
You are old, your memory's poor,
   and little lively me –
Sheila – cook, chum, nurse – far more –
   will set your spirit free.'

Gorgeous girl with flowing hair
Loves to bustle, tidy, care.
'You sit still within your chair,
   it's fun for me to play
Games of housewife, earn my fare
   for travel, which you'll pay.'

Happy girl says cups should hang
Over here. Just so. Crash Bang.
(Rude words are her modern slang.)
   The ancient lady sighs.
Heirlooms, wedding presents, clang
   and shatter. Now she cries.

Carefree girl gets medicines wrong,
Hums a little cheerful song,
Rings the doctor (handsome, strong),
   and flips through the brochures.
Paris, Venice, Greece, Hong Kong.
   This world is full of lures.

Dreaming girl breaks two more plates,
Throws out clothes with holes (she hates
Mending); sometimes she berates
    her patient, when she spills.
'You make me late for all my dates!'
    (Old folk have other ills.)

Brave explorer scrubs and scours,
Milk jug holds a bunch of flowers.
'Dear old lady! Happy hours!'
    'Behave!' Kiss. 'Smile and sit!'
Bye-bye Sheila. Tracey towers.
    She's huge and keen and fit.

Sheila travels – foot, thumb, bus –
Thinks the world is super-plus.
Tummy-trouble, fever, pus
    from jungle-sore and bite.
Tracey meanwhile makes a fuss.
    'Such chaos!' Sets it right.

Big and bouncy Tracey earns
Keep and fare and love. She yearns
Over the old, young, pets, and burns
    for home and motherhood.
Visitors find clean towels, ferns
    in pots, new plates. She's good.

Tracey jogs each afternoon.
Wan explorer knocks. She'll soon
Faint. 'Dear old lady! – Save me!' – Swoon.
    'Sheila? You need some tea.'

– But where are teapot, kettle, spoon?
   All vanished magically.

Sheila seeks the teapot here,
Laura (before her) liked it near,
Back-packing Alice dumped her gear
   and knocked it from the shelf.
'Tracey's paper flowers now cheer
   the bare shelf and myself.'

Starving Sheila tries to find
Cups and cakes. ' – I must be blind!
Everything's changed and moved – unkind!'
   She thinks she hears a moan.
'Often I fear I've lost my mind.
   This home was once my own.'

Sheila remembers when she came,
Making a home from home her aim.
Laura and Alice did the same
   As Tracey has today.
Building a nest is fun, a game
   That all girls like to play.

Ancient lady (boss) has found
Cracked cups, teapot, leather-bound
Copy of Mrs. Beeton, drowned
   In drips below the sink.
She spreads her treasures on the ground
   And crouches down to think.

Tracey is back! Has caught them! Stares.
Crouching old lady? Litter? Glares.
Sheila, inside a cupboard, swears
    And drops a biscuit-tin.
Outraged Tracey weeps, declares
    To spoil her nest is sin.

Crown of her joy, her love, her skill,
Ferns all along the window-sill,
Bull-fighting posters, gingham frill
    On every pot of jam.
Banished old lady, Sheila, will
    Soon learn their nests were sham.

Guilty old lady, dim with doubt,
Guilty young Sheila, tiptoe out,
Creep to a pub, swill sherry, stout
    And port with gloomy zest.
Tracey, triumphant, strides about
    Her home, her realm, her nest.

NURSEY

I

She didn't have a waistline,
More a trunk or torso,
Mass of solid muscle
Packed inside her dress –
Grey or black or navy,
Starched or lacy collar,
Cameo or necklace
Clasping at her neck.

Big round head
Black hair scraped
Small sharp eyes
Pursed up mouth
High clear voice
Strong red hands
Stout in mind and body
With a long loud laugh.

Here comes Nursey,
Jolly old Nursey,
Grown-ups all love Nursey,
She'll never let you down.
Brick, sport, Nursey,
'Best armchair for Nursey',
Grown-ups worship Nursey –
'We'll never let her down.'

2

The children frown
They want to go
Though parents proud
Desire to show
Nursey inspects
With hug and kiss
The children beg
To flee from this
The parents say
Their kids are shy
The children know
The reason why
Escape and hide
Upstairs alone
And only safe
When Nursey's gone.

The children are seeing
A tall house of darkness
A narrow dark staircase
That climbs out of sight
With one child below
Who always looks upward
And one child above
Looking down from the height.

Someone is silent
And someone is shouting
And someone is crying
And something is bleak

As one child looks down
And one child looks upward
Forbidden to reach out,
To touch or to speak.

'There goes Nursey, dearest cheery Nursey,
Isn't she a marvel!' The parents wave goodbye –
There goes Nursey, the children watching Nursey
From an upstairs window, wish that she would die.

3

'In those days, the nightingales sang all night,
In those days, there were picnics by the river,
The green slow river, with everyone dressed in white –
And tennis in white, with daisies on grassy lawns,
The sweetness of scent, honeysuckle, roses,
Friends talking to friends from twilight until dawn.

In those days, courting couples were never
Left alone together, but always were chaperoned
By older, wiser, women who watched for ever –
Except for Nursey, our favourite chaperone,
Knitting, drowsing, closing her eyelids so kindly,
Waking, startled. 'Fancy how time has flown!'

Mother, father, reminisce in the twilight,
'Good old Nursey, fancy how time has flown.'

4

Nursey was there at every wedding
(See her in the photo, right beside the bride),
Nursey was there at every christening
(Making sure the baby was dry and never cried) –
Nursey changed the nappies, Nursey did the mending,
Baked and shopped and gladly pushed the heavy pram,
Boasting of the part she'd played with all the parents
(Nightingales and roses, chaperones a sham).
'Good old Nursey, thinks she owns our babies!'
Angry children mutter 'Nursey is a sham'.

Mother tells the children, 'poor Nursey is no sham.'

5

'Long long ago, our Nursey was Lily,
Orphanage Lily, lacking a family,
Just rules and uniform, punishment, penitence,
Hunger and cold and nowhere to go.

Then came a miracle – Lily was chosen
By a rich couple – elderly – barren –
Christian, and wanting to help a poor orphan.
– How could they do it, not knowing children?

They gave Lily clothes, good food, a nursery,
Also an excellent uniformed Nanny
To teach Lily godliness, manners, obedience,
Cleanliness, thankfulness, sitting up straight.

Each weekday evening, Nanny brought Lily
Down to say prayers with Father and Mother.
Church twice on Sundays, inspection, confession,
Then family tea to seal all was well.

Up in the nursery, excellent Nanny
Taught Lily everything, easily, speedily,

For

Each time Lily
Spilt her milk
Broke a plate
Raised her voice
Nanny said 'Lily
Bad girl Lily
Put your Orphanage
Uniform on.
Lay the table,
Bread and water,
Button up
Your Orphanage coat.
Shame on you Lily,
Such ingratitude –
Back to the Orphanage
Where you belong.'

Lily begged Nanny,
Clutched at her, hugged her,
'Dearest Nanny
I will always be good'.

6

Slowly, slowly, Lily grew taller,
Uniformed Nanny seemed smaller and smaller.

Lily had lessons; she trained as a nurse.
Nanny, unwanted, found other jobs worse.

Lily stayed faithful till both parents died –
She gained house and money but still Lily cried

Till one sunny morning she woke up free.
'I'm Nursey, not Lily, and I will be Me!'

7

Nursey thought her parents' Will had left her safe and
    comfortable
But found when the accounts were checked she'd have to
    earn some more.
First she tried a hospital, a public school, a nursing home,
Then loved the job in college though it left her rather poor.
She couldn't face a prison, it would be too like the
    Orphanage. –
The Orphanage Committee once suggested she apply –
She tore the envelope in two and chose to run a Children's
    Home
In her own home, but nobody was happy. Wondering why,
She remembered her old Nanny who was excellent at
    everything

And taught young Lily godliness, obedience and such
Necessities as cleanliness and sitting straight and gratitude,
It's rather rude to raise your voice, nice people rarely touch
Except when little children sometimes need a slight
    correction –
Yes, Nursey felt that Nanny as a model was the best.
She tried so hard to copy her, to maintain perfect discipline,
Till she recalled how Nanny's discipline had too much zest –
So she settled down to make herself an asset in the
    neighbourhood
With baby-sitting, Granny-sitting, any kind good deed.
She was welcomed by all parents and policemen, also clergy-
    men,
And doctors, teachers, midwives praised her name, declared
    that she'd
Find every door wide open, and everyone would say
Three loud cheers for Nursey, who is on her way.

Yes Nursey is successful, such a friend to all the families
Who tell her every trouble, every secret, every fear.
She seems part of the furniture, her beaming face, her
    jollity –
No-one needs to worry when they know that Nursey's near.

8

Yet –
Nursey's home is dark,
Curtains closed all day,
Rooms are high and large.
Walls are greenish-grey,

Everything is neat,
Everything is clean,
All the silver shines,
Dust is never seen.
Everything is best –
Beds and sofas, chairs –
Everything is old,
Everything is hers.
Everything is still,
Silence everywhere,
Nobody would know
Who is living here
Everything reminds
Nursey of childhood,
Everything recalls
The need for being good.

9

Here comes Nursey,
Jolly old Nursey,
Life and soul of parties,
Always such fun,
In the best armchair and
Dressing like a peacock –
'Would you like another?'
'Just a little one.'
Nursey in her glory,
Close to end of story,
Whispers and cold faces –
Why do people shun

Nursey in her sorrow?
Did she covet? Borrow?
Something of another's?
What has Nursey done?

10

Brave Nursey travels south. She needs a job.
She's found a little flat and joined a club.
She writes to all the friends she used to know
And takes them out to dinner and a show.
She likes to visit, likes to organise,
Assist, inspect, advise and criticise –
But something's changed, she's lost her bounce, her joy,
She's not as loud, she's easier to annoy.
Her clothes are sombre now, she's eating less,
She doesn't seem so packed into her dress.
The grown-up children watch, are torn between
New pity, chill for what she once had been.
Everyone asks (when she at last has gone),
'What did she do, did she let someone down?'

Wiser people wonder, 'did someone let her down?'

11

Nursey invites a grown-up child to dine.
She promises good food and also wine.
Her club, she says, is at a new address.

The child forgets, is late, sees the distress
Of Nursey, far across the empty room,
Alone and old. Says she will visit soon.

12

Where is Nursey?
In a distant suburb,
Lilacs in the garden.
The guest climbs up a hill.
Sees a large white house, named
'Oaklands Nursing Home'. She
Pulls the heavy doorbell.
Are all the inmates ill?

Hears slow footsteps coming.
Nursey's at the door and
Whispers 'Can you manage
Several flights of stairs?'
First a wide white staircase,
Nursey pants, says 'Shh! dear,
Everyone's asleep here,
Wake them if you dare!'

Here's another staircase,
Narrow, leading up to
Higher steps and higher,
Nursey's attic home,
Neat and clean. Tired Nursey,
Pauses, boils a kettle,

Finds a tin of biscuits.
'Friends are not welcome.

They call me Lily here dear,
They all seem rather strict here,
They don't pay me for working
But I'm lucky for my age,
I'm not charged for my room and
They also kindly feed me,
I still have a few savings –
I can manage with no wage.

Would you like a sherry?
Would you like another?'
Nursey winks 'Behold the
Store behind my bed!
What's the work I do here?
You're too young to know dear
I don't think I should tell you.
It is laying out the dead.

Pennies on their eyelids,
Things that I won't mention.
It happens here so often,
It sometimes gets me down –
At my age I am close to
Being dead myself soon.
Hard to sleep at nights now.'
Nursey stops a frown.

'So kind of you to come here,'
They creep down every staircase

In the sleeping house, then
Softly cross the floor.
Nursey puts a finger
To her lips, blows kisses,
Winks again, 'goodbye dear,'
Shuts the heavy door.

A PLEASANT LADY IN BLUE

'You didn't know me, did you?
Have you forgotten last year?'
Said a pleasant lady in blue.

'I'm Rosie – remember? – who
You sent to the loony-bin dear.
You didn't know me, did you?

I'd collapsed on the sofa, due
To some smokes and some drinks. – I felt queer!'
Said a pleasant lady in blue.

'And the sofa had burnt a bit too,
And Ron said he'd kill me, for fear
(You didn't know me, did you?)

Of my killing the kids first, in view
Of my habits. The kids were somewhere –'
Said a pleasant lady in blue,

'So we each got locked up! Which led to
This consequence – my boyfriend here.
You didn't know me, did you?'
Said a pleasant lady in blue.

TWO AND A HALF

I'm two and a half years old,
I'm the baby and clap my hands –
When my brothers and mother scream at each other
Baby can understand
That while I am two and a half,
And while I clap my hands,
My brothers and mother and father will cuddle
And kiss me and hold my hands.

I am nearly three years old.
There's a baby I cuddle and kiss.
When my mother and father and brothers are swearing
And fall on the floor, I know this –
That while I am nearly three,
And while I cuddle and kiss,
My brothers and father and mother may struggle
But I'll still be safe while I kiss.

I am three and a half years old,
I clap my hands and laugh
When my brothers fight and my father hits
And my mother cries, I laugh –
I can be safe when I laugh
While I am three and a half.
They won't want to slap me, they'll kiss me and cuddle me
While I stay three and a half.

THE CHILDREN'S HOME

I have fifteen children to wake up and wash and dress and take
to the loo,
Fifteen children with mealtimes and playtimes and bathtimes
and bedtimes – could you
Care for fifteen children, some boys some girls, some dark
some fair – can you see
Why I cuddle Rosie, fat blue-eyed Rosie, who runs to sit on
my knee?

NEARLY FOUR

I am nearly four years old
And this is my new home.
There aren't any smells or scuffles or yells
And the strangers say 'Welcome' to me.

Welcome?

I'm the baby and nearly four.
I clap hands and I sit on their knees
I cuddle and kiss and remember this –
That if I can really please

They will be nice to me –
They'll all be nice to me.
While I'm their baby to cuddle and kiss
Of course they'll be nice to me –

But when I reach four or five or more,
Will they still be nice to me?

THE LITTLE GIRL

We took into our home a little girl,
We thought she'd like to come,
Our offer seemed so handsome,
We wanted to share our home.

She took to us at once, the little girl,
She'd clap her hands and dance,
And kiss and cuddle, entrance
Our days with her skyblue glance.

She took us in, I fear, that little girl.
Our daughter learnt to swear,
Our treasures would disappear,
Our boys kissed, cuddled, hugged her.

So she was taken back, poor little girl.
She made us want to smack,
Shout, fight. We hadn't the knack
Of loving enough. Our lack.

THE BEDROOM

I used to have a bedroom of my very very own,
I kept it just the way I liked, I never felt alone,
I had my dolls to dress and feed, my dolls' house and my
    bear,
My picture books and china dogs. Then Rosie came to share.

My Mummy said that Rosie's home was not a bit like mine,
She'd a mother and a father and two brothers which was
    fine
But she'd never had enough to eat, nor clothes, nor toys
    for play,
So all of us must welcome her and make her want to stay.

The first day Rosie came to us she sat on Mummy's knee
And Daddy told her stories like the ones he tells to me,
My two big brothers petted her and Mummy said that I
Must treat her as a sister, but I didn't want to try.

They made me share my bedroom with poor Rosie, who
    would take
My favourite doll to bed with her, and tear my books, and
    break
My tiny dolls' house furniture, and blind my teddy bear
By tugging at his button eyes. I wished she wasn't there,

So I pinched her when she grabbed my doll, or when she
    told a lie
And said that I had hit her – which I hadn't – then she'd cry

And they took sides with Rosie till one day they heard her
      swear
And soon I learnt her language and we both swore everywhere

And I told Rosie secret things and she told me some more,
And jokes I told my brothers which they told their friends,
      and poor
Rosie had to leave us when we found she'd hidden away
Some treasures and some bits of food. So Rosie couldn't stay

And in fact I quite missed Rosie, it was quite fun being bad
Till my parents were quite angry and they told me to be sad.
They still see Rosie sometimes, and sometimes they let me
      go,
And though we've grown quite differently, I envy Rosie so.

DRINKING SONG

(Tune: Begone Dull Care)

My wife says I
      am to blame for their taking the kids,
But I say I
      can't be blamed if I don't earn quids.
It's thanks to her that we live in a sty,
               she lazes about all day,
But I swear I
      am disgusted we live this way.

My man says I
      am the one who should take the blame,
And my man says I
      am the cause that the Council came.
When he gets a drink he fancies a fight,
               so I gave the Council his name
When someone complained of the row that night,
      and there had to be someone to blame.

The days seem long
      without children who scream and scrap,
The days seem long
      without children to hug or slap.
She's cleaned up the house till there's nothing wrong,
               and he's got a job again,
But without any children the days are so long,
               we'll drink together again.

THE CONFERENCE

A Conference. Biscuits and tea
In the Staff Room. The Chairman says 'We
Have failed with this child
Who is now running wild.
I remember her once, on my knee,

A plump blue-eyed angel. Her home
Was quite filthy – no toothbrush, no comb,
No soap, broom or brush,
The loo wouldn't flush,
Untrained dogs round your feet. The outcome

Was Substitute Care – fostering
In our very best home, offering
Happy family life,
No swearing, no strife –
Fresh start, second chance, everything.

A disaster! They sent her away,
Though they still keep in touch to this day.
She came here, improved,
Went home, was removed.
Now nobody wants her to stay."

Rosie says, 'Can I speak? May I go
To my real Mum and Dad?' 'They say no.
You're too posh for them there,
And they've no room to spare,
And you're almost a stranger you know.'

THE SOCIAL WORKERS' POLKA

(tune: You Should See Me Dance the Polka)

'I had luck with Doreen Davies,'
'I could talk to Nicholas Black,'
'Then they gave you pale Miss Busby,'
'Then we all shared Uncle Jack.'
'How we hated Mrs. Morgan,'
'How we loved that student Jim,'
'As for jolly old Uncle Stanley –
Well we all had trouble with him.'

'Then they swapped your Doreen Davies
For my gorgeous Nicholas Black,'
'And when pale Miss Busby fainted,
Was it love for Uncle Jack?'
'Then the lot of us got Mrs. Morgan
When we longed for student Jim,'
'And jolly old Uncle Stanley –
Something curious happened with him.'

'Then they changed our social workers
When they moved the Counties around,'
'And I ended up with Miss Hislop
When brave Miss Baxter was drowned,'
'And you won Matilda Wilson –'
'Auntie Tilly was fun –'
'But how about fat Sister Betty
Who terrified everyone?'

'Then that silly Miss Hislop married
And motherly Mabel came
And stayed for years, God bless her!'
'My kind Mr. Gifford was lame.'
'Dear Auntie Tilly left me
When Uncle Stanley came back –'
'Was it Carol who ran for shelter
Sixty miles to our Uncle Jack?'

'I will never forget Mrs. Davies,'
'And we'll always remember Jim,'
'I get cards from Mrs. Cartwright,'
'But who discovered Miss Pym?'
'Uncle Jack has to be favourite,'
'Though the boys all adore Miss McPhail.'
'I hope Sister Betty is burning.'
'At least Uncle Stanley's in jail.'

PUBLIC LIFE

Public houses, public parks, public meetings in public
    places,
Public lavatories, public baths, public servants with public
    faces,
Public libraries, public worship, public school and
    publications
Publishing the public-spirited affairs of public people for
    our recreation.

– But if you'd lived in public since the age of two,
With files as thick as wedding-cakes written about you,
Conferences, supervisors, court reports – you'd sigh
And want a bit of privacy before you die.

SIXTEEN

I am sixteen today,
Sweet sixteen today,
I haven't a house or a key or a door
But at last I'm sixteen and for evermore
I am free to do what I like!
Try and stop me! I'll do what I like!
Though I haven't a bed to sleep in tonight
I am free! I am sixteen today!

ROSIE'S STORY OR STORIES

(children's hymn – Tell Me the Stories of Jesus)

'I'll tell you my story or stories,
Your turn to hear
Just what it's like to be Rosie,
Rosie's career –
Born in a pigsty,
Raised in a zoo,
If I would love them
They'd love me too.

One night my Mummy and Daddy
Scrapped on the floor,
Baby was screaming her head off,
Both parents swore,
In came the strangers,
Mouths full of blame,
Drove me through darkness –
Never the same.

Next there were hundreds of children
Round Nursey's knee,
I got there first with my kisses,
Nursey loved me,
Chose little Rosie
Best foster home,
Till they discovered
Their treasures gone.

Dear little, poor little Rosie,
Blue-eyed and sweet

Can't be a dolly all day, though
People cry 'Cheat!'
Sometimes it's language,
Sometimes it's theft,
Sometimes behaviour
Leaves her bereft.

School after school after school, and
Home, Convent, Home
Spoil blue-eyed Rosie their darling,
Then want her gone –
Even the pigsty,
Family zoo,
Find her too posh now –
Goodbye to you.

Streets are the best place for friendship
Though wet and cold
Hostels and prisons can teach things
School never told.
Rosie's the expert,
Drink, drugs and hugs
Till babies cry and
Kind hearts are tugged.

What was it like being Rosie?
My parents' child?
One of a crowd in Care? Or
Fostered and mild?
Wise on the streets?
A home of my own
Like Mum and Dad's, where
Troubles are known?

TWO OF ROSIE'S CHILDREN, IN THE NEXT ROOM

(nursery rhyme: The Brave Old Duke of York)

We don't like our home,
Nothing ever seems right,
Our Mum and Dad often laugh and sing,
Next minute they swear and fight.
Our Mum goes sick and strange,
Our Dad gets heavy with his hand,
The two of us try to keep things right
But we're scared of her eyes and his hand.

Our Mum didn't like her home,
Her parents drank and fought,
Her Mum never cooked or mended or scrubbed
Because she'd never been taught.
She says they were strapped for cash,
Her Dad couldn't hold any job,
He was proud to be the man his father was
So he drank and fought and lost each job.

Our Nan who comes to stay
Tells us she's not to blame –
'If you're strapped for cash then living is hard,
The wide world over it's the same.'
Her parents who are dead and are gone
Didn't have the same advantages as us,
The one was in an orphanage the other in a war
So they neither knew a home like us.

Our Nan didn't like her home,
Nor Dad nor our Dad's Nan,
They say there's always war or you're out of work,
You must lead your life as you can.
Our Mum was taken away,
They made her posh and grand,
She says she isn't fish nor fowl any more –
Shall we stay or become too grand?

We don't like our home,
Nothing ever seems right,
Though our Mum and our Dad often laugh and often sing
Next minute they'll swear and fight.
When I grow will I look like Mum?
When I grow will I look like Dad?
We're frightened to stay and we're frightened to go
Or turning into Mum and Dad.

A PLEASANT LADY IN BLUE

Reprise

'You didn't know me, did you?
Have you forgotten last year?'
Said a pleasant lady in blue.

'I'm Rosie – remember? – who
You sent to the loony-bin dear.
You didn't know me, did you?

I'd collapsed on the sofa, due
To some smokes and some drinks. – I felt queer!'
Said a pleasant lady in blue.

'And the sofa had burnt a bit too,
And Ron said he'd kill me, for fear
(You didn't know me, did you?)

Of my killing the kids first, in view
Of my habits. The kids were somewhere –'
Said a pleasant lady in blue,

'So we each got locked up. Which led to
This consequence – my boyfriend here.
He's a fireman. I trust him, he's true.'
Said the pleasant lady in blue.

THE FRESH START

(continuing Rosie's story in boyfriend's voice)

'Rosie has told me her story,'
Says Keith the true,
'Story or stories, I trust her,
Dear girl in blue –
Nothing but hardship
Yet she's all heart,
You'll find you're wrong, we'll
Make a fresh start.'

(Both voices)

'You'll find you're wrong, we'll
Make a fresh start.'